Wrestling Greats

STING

Ross Davies

Union Public Library

The Rosen Publishing Group, Inc.
New York

Published in 2002 by The Rosen Publishing Group, Inc.
29 East 21st Street, New York, NY 10010

Copyright © 2002 by The Rosen Publishing Group, Inc.

First Edition

Library of Congress Cataloging-in-Publication Data

Davies, Ross.
Sting / by Ross Davies. — 1st ed.
p. cm. — (Wrestling greats)
Includes bibliographical references (p.) and index.
Summary: Examines the performing techniques, athletic
ability, and career of the wrestler known as Sting.
ISBN 0-8239-3490-X
1. Sting (Wrestler), 1959– —Juvenile literature.
2. Wrestlers—United States—Biography—Juvenile literature.
[1. Sting (Wrestler), 1959– 2. Wrestlers.]
I. Title. II. Series.
GV1196.S75 D38 2001
796.812'.092—dc21
2001002696

Manufactured in the United States of America

Contents

Fiercely private, Sting is something of an enigma in the world of wrestling, which is dominated by self-promoters.

The Rise to Stardom

He is a mystery in face paint. Although he has been a public figure since 1985, no one really knows much about Sting. He has protected his privacy as closely as he has protected his reputation, only teasing us with occasional glimpses behind the mask he has created for himself. There is no superstar athlete about whom so little is known. When the announcers dramatically shout, "This is Sting!" are they sure who he is exactly?

The man who the wrestling world would come to know as Sting was born Steve Borden on March 20, 1959, in Omaha, Nebraska. Soon after, his family moved to Venice Beach, California, where young Borden immersed himself in the southern California lifestyle: beaches, sports, and lifting weights. He was a natural athlete who participated in a number of sports, including basketball, swimming, and amateur wrestling. In fact, several of Borden's family members were amateur wrestlers.

Borden was one of the best athletes in his high school, and he could have gone on to play sports at the elite college of his choice, but he was not interested in competing in the more traditional college sports like football. At age fifteen, Borden was walking past Gold's Gym in downtown Venice Beach. He walked in and saw hundreds of huge, muscular men pumping iron. Borden was entranced. With his parents' permission, he joined the club and embarked on a rigorous power-lifting and weight-training schedule.

In his senior year of high school, Borden turned down numerous scholarship offers from top colleges in the country so that he could concentrate on bodybuilding. Instead, he attended a junior college (a two-year school), where he played basketball and continued to lift weights. In 1984, Borden was one point short of qualifying for the Mr. USA competition, the most important body-building competition in the country.

Borden and gymmate Jim Hellwig —who would come to be known to the wrestling world as the Ultimate Warrior—were working out at Gold's Gym in Venice Beach when they were discovered by former pro wrestler Red Bastien. Bastien, a wrestling star in the 1960s, convinced Borden and Hellwig to give pro wrestling a try. They agreed, and Bastien put them through two months of rigorous training.

Bastien, along with aspiring manager Rick Bassman, formed a team called Powerslam USA, which consisted of four young, muscular wrestlers, including

Borden and Hellwig. Borden took on the ring name Flash. Hellwig became known as Rock. Powerslam USA made its ring debut on November 1, 1985, in Las Vegas, Nevada, but the team fell apart when two other members decided to leave the sport.

But Flash and Rock worked well together and immediately fascinated the fans in Mid-South Wrestling, which would become known as the Universal Wrestling Federation, or UWF. Competing without the help of their former teammates or Bastien and Bassman, the duo became known as the Blade Runners. They wore colorful face paint and instilled excitement in the growing wrestling federation with their youth, impressive physiques, and ability to intimidate opponents. They won their debut match as the Blade Runners in only forty-five seconds, and before long, announcers were billing Flash as "every man's nightmare." Unfortunately, Borden and Hellwig were living a nightmare of their own.

"We had so little money when we first started training with Red Bastien that we got caught one night in a grocery store eating Colby cheese in the aisle," Hellwig recalled. "They caught us just as we had a mouthful of that dry cheese. We both ran so far and so fast that both of us thought we were going to have to perform CPR [cardiopulmonary resuscitation] on one another."

The Blade Runners didn't last long. Hellwig left the UWF to become a singles wrestler in another organization. Flash stayed in the Mid-South on his own and changed his name to Sting. He was without his tag team partner and without Bastien and Bassman. He was alone and vulnerable, easy prey for someone who didn't have his best interests at heart. That person turned out to be "Hot Stuff"

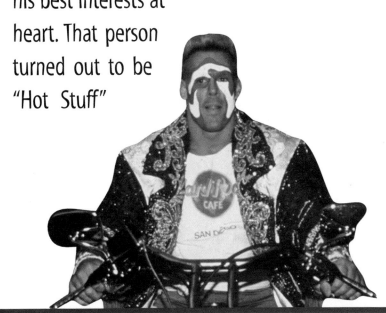

Eddie Gilbert, a loudmouthed wrestler-manager whose rulebreaking ways were wreaking havoc on the UWF. Gilbert convinced Sting to join Hot Stuff International, his stable of wrestlers that also included future World Championship Wrestling (WCW) star Rick Steiner.

At first, Sting and Gilbert were successful. On July 20, 1986, they won the UWF tag team championship from the Fantastics (Tommy Rogers and Bobby Fulton). Gilbert and Sting were then stripped of their belts after a match against the Fantastics on August 17, 1986, but they regained the belts in a rematch. On September 27, 1986, the Fantastics regained the title yet again and ended the feud.

The fans hated Gilbert and Sting. Their illegal tactics and arrogant attitudes made them the most detested team in the UWF. But Sting was getting noticed. At the end of 1986, the readers of *Pro Wrestling Illustrated* magazine voted Sting second runner-up for Rookie of the Year. He finished behind Lex Luger and Bam Bam Bigelow.

Sting and Gilbert, however, were not getting along. Sting was angry that Gilbert seemed more interested in impressing Missy Hyatt (the beautiful wrestling manager who had recently dumped her boyfriend) than in doing things for the benefit of Hot Stuff International. The tension between Sting and Gilbert grew as their team's effectiveness decreased. On February 7, 1987, Sting and Gilbert lost to Terry Taylor and Chris Adams in the final round of a tournament for the vacant UWF tag team title. Sting and Rick Steiner won the belts from Taylor and Adams on April 12, 1987, but the end of Sting's alliance with Hot Stuff International was near.

On May 17, Sting and Steiner defended the UWF tag belts against Brad Armstrong and Tim Horner. During the match, Gilbert climbed onto the ring apron and went to hit Armstrong. Armstrong, however, ducked out of the way, and Gilbert struck Sting instead. Armstrong and Horner won the match and the belts, and Sting's relationship with Hot Stuff International was over.

Backed by the fans' cheers, Sting went after his former teammates, who were ruthless in their attempts to destroy him. On August 3, 1987, Sting was scheduled to wrestle Gilbert, who had won the UWF television title. But Terry Taylor, who had recently joined Hot Stuff International, ambushed Sting and hit him over the head with a chair.

Blood poured down Sting's face. Fifteen stitches were needed to close the wound, and Sting had no choice but to back out of the match. A wrestler named Shane Douglas took his place, and Sting's assistance helped Douglas beat Gilbert

Sting savors victory while the defeated Ric Flair kisses the mat.

for the belt. It was sweet revenge but certainly not sweet enough. Sting wanted the title for himself.

But Sting never got the chance. In late 1987, the powerful National Wrestling Alliance (NWA), one of the two biggest wrestling federations in North America, bought the UWF. Sting, a rising star, was one of the main reasons the NWA wanted the UWF. NWA wrestler Ric Flair noticed the league's interest in Sting. Flair had recently lost the NWA world title to Ronnie Garvin on September 25, 1987.

At that point, Flair was a five-time former world champion and was perhaps the best all-around wrestler in the world.

Sting's outgoing personality, flamboyant costumes, and confidence in the ring won him many fans, especially young ones.

Flair was so worried about Sting that he had members of his rulebreaking clique, the Four Horsemen, try to defeat Sting. Lex Luger of the Horsemen wrestled Sting in several matches, with neither man gaining a clear advantage. On November 26, 1987, in Chicago, Illinois, Sting made his pay-per-view debut at the NWA's most important card of the year: Starrcade. He teamed with Ronnie Garvin and Michael Hayes and wrestled Gilbert, Steiner, and Larry Zbyszko to a sixty-minute draw. That same night, in another match, Flair regained the NWA world title from Ronnie Garvin.

Fans around the world began to notice Sting. He was a superstar in the making.

2 Taking on the Horsemen

There was nothing fluky about Sting's quick rise to stardom. After all, he had everything going for him: youth, athletic ability, a great physique, and colorful face paint that fascinated the fans. He had an effusive, outgoing personality that came through loud and clear during television interviews. Best of all, despite his inexperience, he was brash, confident, and willing to take on the best wrestlers in the world.

Sting wasted no time taking aim at the NWA world title. A confrontation with J. J. Dillon, Ric Flair's manager, proved to be fortunate. One night after a match, Dillon threw a glass of champagne in Sting's face. Sting attacked Dillon and tried to tear him to pieces until the Four Horsemen saved the manager.

Flair, wanting to avenge the attack on his manager, granted Sting a title shot. They wrestled on December 12, 1987, and Flair prevailed even though he used an illegal move: He held on to the ropes while pinning Sting. Wrestling rules prohibit a wrestler from having any part of his body on or under the ropes while attempting a pin.

They met again in February. Flair was relentless. He punished Sting with eye gouges, punches, and illegal chokeholds, in which a wrestler wraps his hands around an opponent's throat and chokes him. Flair retained his title in a ferocious battle. But after the match, Sting placed Flair in his scorpion death lock, a submission hold in which he uses his legs to tie up his opponent's legs, turns him over, and applies painful pressure to the lower back. Sting held Flair in the hold for several minutes, and the champion had to be taken away on a stretcher. The crowd loved it.

Their next high-profile clash came on March 27, 1988, in the main event of the NWA's first Clash of the Champions telecast

Sting and Randy Savage made an imposing wrestling team.

from Greensboro, North Carolina. A special stipulation of the match was that it could not end in a draw; there had to be a winner. Five judges sat at ringside to decide on the match in case the forty-five-minute time limit expired without a decision. Sting and Flair threw everything they had at each other, but neither man could be beaten. When the bell rang ending the match, both men were still standing.

The NWA world title hung in the balance. One judge voted for Sting, while the next voted for Flair. Another judge voted for Sting, and another voted for Flair. The score was tied at two. The fifth judge ruled the match a draw, giving Flair the championship by default (Sting had to beat Flair to gain the title). Flair had retained the title by the narrowest possible margin. Although the outcome frustrated Sting, who felt he had beaten Flair, the match was further proof of his status as a rising star. Sting would not need any more proof after April 23, 1988.

Lex Luger, who had left the Four Horsemen shortly after Starrcade '87, had recently been betrayed by his tag team partner, Barry Windham. Suddenly, Luger was without a partner for the 1988 Jim Crockett Memorial Cup tag team tournament, on April 22 in Greensville, South Carolina, and on April 23 in Greensboro, North Carolina. The Crockett Memorial Cup, with its $1 million first prize, featured the greatest tag teams in the world in a two-day single-elimination tournament.

Luger convinced Sting to be his part-ner, and they clicked immediately. After receiving a bye in the first round, Luger and Sting beat Dick Murdoch and Ivan Koloff. In the quarterfinals, they beat the Midnight Express, the team of Bobby Eaton and Stan Lan. In the semifinals, they beat Barbarian and Warlord. In the championship round, they beat Tully Blanchard and Arn Anderson of the Horsemen. This newly formed team had prevailed against the best in the game and had won $1 million.

Sting spent the rest of 1988 making his mark on the NWA. He was voted Most Improved Wrestler of 1988 and finished third behind Randy Savage and Hulk Hogan for Most Popular Wrestler. His match against Flair at the Clash of the Champions finished second for Match of the Year.

The year 1989 would be an eventful one for Sting. In March, NWA television champion Mike Rotundo offered Sting the belt and $10,000 if he could pin him in ten minutes or less. Sting did it. Then, on May 7, 1989, at the Music City Showdown in Nashville, Tennessee, Sting retained the title by beating former World Wrestling Federation (WWF) world heavyweight champion the Iron Sheik in just over two minutes. At the Great American Bash on July 23, 1989, in Baltimore, Maryland, Sting appeared to have pinned the Great Muta.

But video replays later showed that Muta had lifted his shoulder before the three-count. The title was upheld.

That night, however, was notable for a more important reason. In the main event, Flair defended the world title against long-time nemesis Terry Funk. After Flair pinned Funk to retain the title, Muta stormed the ring and attacked Flair. Much to everyone's amazement, Sting came to Flair's rescue. They shook hands and forged a friendship. At Halloween Havoc on October 28, 1989, in Philadelphia, Sting and Flair teamed to beat Funk and Muta.

Considering their past relationship, the friendship between Flair and Sting seemed shaky. It turned shakier when Ole and Arn Anderson returned to the NWA and said they wanted to reunite Flair's old team, the Four Horsemen. On December 13, 1989, at Starrcade in Atlanta, Sting, Muta, Flair, and Luger competed in a four-man Iron Man tournament. The tournament consisted of one-on-one bouts involving the four men.

Luger pinned Sting in the first match. Sting came back to pin Muta in his second match. Flair and Luger battled to a draw, then Luger beat Muta by disqualification. Sting needed to beat Flair in the final bout to win the tournament. He did, pinning Flair in less than sixteen minutes. But when the match ended, the Andersons entered the ring. Would they attack Sting? Would Sting's

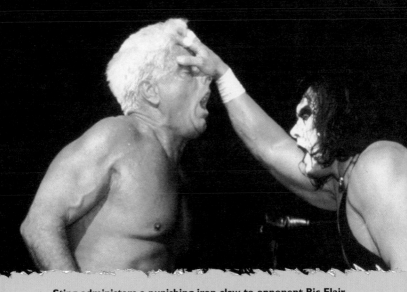
Sting administers a punishing iron claw to opponent Ric Flair.

friendship with Flair come to a painful conclusion? As it tuned out, no. Flair and the Andersons congratulated Sting. And on January 2, 1990, Sting was introduced as the newest member of the Four Horsemen.

"Sting is finally being rewarded for being one of the best wrestlers in our sport," Flair said. But the potential for conflict was enormous. Flair was the NWA world champion, and Sting wanted to be world champion. And the promoters, who make money signing matches that fans will pay to see, wanted more Sting versus Flair.

The other three Horsemen were enraged when Sting demanded a shot at the world title. Their rage turned to blind fury when the NWA announced that Sting would battle Flair for the world title at Wrestle War '90 on February 25 in Greensboro, North Carolina. The Andersons and Flair confronted Sting at Clash of the Champions on February 6, 1990, in Corpus Christi, Texas, where they all had matches. The Andersons and Flair demanded that Sting give up the title match scheduled later that month.

"You did the one unforgivable thing that we can never forget," said Ole Anderson. "When you signed that match to meet Ric Flair on February 26, you signed your death warrant. You're not going to be a Horseman anymore. That's it. You're finished as a Horseman."

Later that night at Clash of the Champions, Flair and the Andersons wrestled the Great Muta, Dragon Master, and Buzz Sawyer in a cage match, which is a match fought entirely within a steel cage. During the match, Sting climbed to the top of the cage. Security guards ran out and pulled Sting down. He fell to the floor. On impact, Sting felt pain tearing through his knee. The injury was diagnosed as a torn left kneecap. Sting would have to undergo major surgery. He'd be out of action for six months.

The timing could not have been worse. Not only was Sting no longer a member of the Horsemen, but he also could not wrestle Flair at Wrestle War. Luger got the chance instead, and Sting showed up to cheer him on from ringside. But thirty-eight minutes into the match, the Andersons attacked Sting. Luger left the ring to rescue his friend and was counted out.

Once again, the Horsemen's evil deeds had saved Flair. He remained world champion. Sting, however, refused to be denied. He watched from the sidelines and waited, confident that his day would come.

3 The Glory Days

t's never easy for a pro wrestler to sit on the sidelines and wait. It's even more difficult for a man who was on the verge of glory to have his chance taken away by the shenanigans of others. Sting, however, had no choice but to watch. He cheered on Luger. He often came to the ring with Luger for Luger's matches, only to get attacked by the Four Horsemen. The Horsemen unleashed a particularly heinous attack on Sting at Capital Combat on May 19, 1990, in Washington, D.C.

"Nobody can ever accuse me of not being a thinking champion," Flair said. "A lot of people are saying that I take advantage of the rules and regulations, but as far as I'm concerned, that's what they're in the books for. All that matters is that I remain world champion."

Perhaps Sting was taking too many chances. After all, doctors considered his injury to be career-threatening. But Sting got into another skirmish with Flair at Clash of the Champions XI in Charleston, South Carolina.

"I want my chance so bad," Sting told Flair that night. "Please, I'm begging you. I don't care when. Let's sign another world title match. It's about my time. I will get down on my knees and beg you. The world title means just as much to me as it does you. Probably more."

Sting returned to the ring on July 1, 1990, in Farmland, Indiana. He teamed with Luger to defeat Flair and Barry Windham, the newest member of the Horsemen. Hoping to stave off the Horsemen's interference, Sting formed a group of his own: the Dudes with Attitudes, which also included Junkyard Dog, Paul Orndorff, and Rick and Scott Steiner. On July 7, 1990, Sting got his long-awaited title shot against Flair at the Great American Bash in Baltimore, Maryland.

Hoping to eliminate the interference by the Horsemen that had cost Luger a fair shot at the world title at Capital Combat, NWA vice president Jim Herd issued several edicts for the bout. The no disqualification rule was waived, meaning that if Flair got disqualified, he'd lose the title.

"But I don't believe there's a chance of that happening because I'm allowing Junkyard Dog, Rick and Scott Steiner, and Paul Orndorff to remain stationed at ringside for the match," Herd said. "This will be a fair one-on-one encounter. May the best man win."

Ric Flair and Sting battle it out in
one of their many grudge matches.

HOGAN
LIKES TO
KODA!

Sting painted his face red, white, and blue in honor of Independence Day. The Dudes were at ringside for Sting. The Horsemen were at ringside for Flair. Sting tore into Flair from the opening bell and rocked the champion with a hard clothesline. Flair fought back, but Sting was seemingly impervious to pain. Early in the match, Sting tested his knee by lifting Flair for a slam. His knee didn't buckle, and he slammed Flair to the canvas.

"From that point on, I knew the match was mine," Sting said. "When I saw the look in Flair's eyes after I slammed him, I knew that he just couldn't believe that I could be back at full strength again. I knew there wasn't a thing he could do to put me down."

Sting administers a scorpion death lock to Ric Flair during one of their many battles.

Late in the match, Sting placed Flair in his scorpion death lock. When the Horsemen tried to attack Sting, the Dudes stopped them. Flair took advantage of the distraction and knocked down Sting, then tried to pin him while both of his feet were on top of the ropes. Scott Steiner pushed Flair's feet off the ropes.

Flair backed Sting into a corner and jarred him with several chops to the chest. Sting whipped Flair into the opposite turnbuckle, but Flair moved out of the way of a Stinger splash, a flying maneuver in which Sting leaps on another wrestler. Sting's bad knee smashed into the turnbuckle. Flair moved in. Sixteen minutes into the match, both men were tiring. Flair grabbed Sting's left leg and spun him around for a figure-four leglock. But Sting reached up, grabbed Flair's left arm, pulled him down to the mat, and covered him for the pin. Sting had won his first NWA world title!

It was a great moment for Sting. The Dudes embraced him in the ring. The crowd broke out in a raucous celebration. Sting was humble in victory.

"I've said it before, but Flair is the greatest world champion of all time," Sting said. "Don't pinch me. I've got to be dreaming!" He had reason to be humble. Months earlier, his career had nearly been ended.

"Hey, I had my doubts, too," Sting told *Pro Wrestling Illustrated* magazine. "Some of the doctors I saw before my surgery said I'd be foolish to go back in that ring. But what good is living without wrestling? And how would I be able to live knowing that it was Flair that put me out of action forever? No way, dude. There was nothing on this earth that was going to stop me from fulfilling my destiny."

Not only was Sting a working champion, but he also teamed with Luger to beat the Horsemen in several tag team bouts. On August 3, 1990, in Greensboro, North Carolina, Sting pinned Flair in their first rematch. At Clash of the Champions XII on September 5 in Asheville, North Carolina, Sting pinned a masked mystery man who called himself the Black Scorpion. Sting pulled off the Scorpion's mask, hoping to find out the man's identity, but another mask was underneath. Sting seemed to be psyched out when he turned around and saw a much larger Black Scorpion standing on the ramp leading to the ring.

The Horsemen did everything in their power to destroy Sting. Sid Vicious joined the Horsemen and was given a shot at Sting at Halloween Havoc on October 27, 1990, in Chattanooga, Tennessee. Vicious dominated the match and pinned Sting. But after the match, the real Sting stumbled out to the ring. The Horsemen had tied him up and left him at the back of the arena. The "Sting" who was pinned by Vicious was actually Barry Windham. When the match restarted, the real Sting pinned Vicious.

Sting reaches for the ropes in an attempt to break out of a submission hold.

Sting and the Black Scorpion met again at Starrcade '90 on December 16 in St. Louis, Missouri. Sting wrestled another outstanding match and pinned the Scorpion in eighteen minutes and thirty-one seconds. Afterward, he unmasked the Scorpion and revealed Ric Flair!

This was an amazing run by Sting. The previous six times Flair had lost the

NWA world title, he had regained it shortly afterward. But Sting was resilient. He was a true champion who won one match after another. The readers of *Pro Wrestling Illustrated* named him Wrestler of the Year.

Only a mistake by the referee cost Sting the world title on January 11, 1991, in East Rutherford, New Jersey. Late in the match, Sting covered Flair for at least four seconds, but referee Nick Patrick had been knocked out during a skirmish. Sting continued his assault, battering Flair with punches and kicks. He then whipped Ric "the Nature Boy" Flair into the ropes. Flair bounded off the ropes and collided with Sting in the center of the ring. Dazed, Sting fell to the mat. Flair dropped on top of him.

Patrick, who was regaining consciousness, inched his way toward the wrestlers and made the count. But he didn't see that Sting had his left foot draped over the second rope. According to the rules, Patrick—if he had noticed the infraction—should have made the wrestlers break apart. Instead, Patrick made the three-count and gave Flair the world title.

"My foot was clearly on the ropes," Sting told *Pro Wrestling Illustrated Weekly*. "Patrick was half out of it, and he was in no shape to count that pinfall. When Patrick got KO'd [knocked out], the officials really should have stopped the bout. But I'm not going to cry or complain about it. I'm just going to work harder than ever to regain the title. I'm making a promise to all my fans that I'm gonna get that belt back."

The loss was extremely difficult for Sting to take. He knew that he hadn't lost the match legally, but pro wrestling doesn't have a procedure for reviewing videotapes, and he had to live with the outcome. But losing the world champion title was tougher. Winning it had given Sting a taste of glory. He knew what it was like to be on top of the wrestling world. But climbing back would not prove easy.

4 Regaining the World Title

Although Sting and Flair had several intense rematches, Sting couldn't win back the title. On January 14, 1991, in Charleston, West Virginia, Flair was disqualified for throwing Sting over the top rope. Since the title could change hands only on a pinfall or a submission, Flair kept the belt. Before long, Sting found himself getting squeezed out of the title picture.

At SuperBrawl I on May 19, 1991, in St. Petersburg, Florida, Japanese star Tatsumi Fujinami had the main event title shot against Flair. Sting teamed with Luger and lost to World Championship Wrestling (WCW) world tag team champions Rick and Scott Steiner (the NWA had recently changed its name to World Championship Wrestling). The match would be voted Match of the Year by the readers of *Pro Wrestling Illustrated*.

During the match, Russian strong-man Nikita Koloff interfered and tried to hit Luger with a chain, but he struck Sting instead. Two months later at the Great American Bash in Baltimore, Sting lost to Koloff in a chain match. And when Flair,

Sting prepares to
inflict damage on an
opponent by jumping
off the top rope.

embroiled in a contract dispute with WCW officials, was stripped of the title, Luger and Barry Windham were named the top two contenders to the world championship. Luger won the belt.

So, with Luger on top of the wrestling world, Sting concentrated on trying to win WCW's second most important title, the U. S. championship. The title had been declared vacant after Luger won the world title (at the time in WCW, a wrestler wasn't allowed to hold two singles championships). The title was placed up for grabs in a one-night tournament on August 25, 1991, in Atlanta, Georgia. In the final round, Sting faced future World Wrestling Federation (WWF) superstar Steve Austin. Lady Blossom, Austin's manager, interfered, but Sting won anyway by pinning Austin.

"I'm proud to be the new U.S. champion, and I'll defend this belt with everything I've got," Sting said. "And then, when I'm considered the best U.S. champion ever, I'll take back the WCW world title from Luger."

But glory was short-lived. On November 19, 1991, in Savannah, Georgia, Sting lost the U.S. title to Rick Rude. Luger attacked Sting during that match and slammed Sting's knee against the ramp. Sting screamed out in pain, but Luger was merciless in his assault on his former friend and brutalized Sting's knee. When Luger was done, Sting had to be taken to a nearby hospital.

Wrestling on his injured knee, Sting lost to Rick Steamboat, then lost in several title shots against Rude, due to interference by Rude's manager, Paul E. Dangerously. But Sting's focus was on Luger, the WCW world title, and the chance to get revenge on the man who injured him while regaining the belt he wanted. He got his chance at SuperBrawl II on February 29, 1992, in Milwaukee, Wisconsin.

During the weeks leading up to the pay-per-view match, Luger went into seclusion with manager Harley Race to train for the match. Sting, despite his bad knee, wrestled in several grueling tag team matches. Luger was a rested man, but when the opening bell rang, Sting was ready.

"What's your problem?
Do something!
Come at me!"

-Sting to Lex Luger

Sting and Luger stared each other down. After two minutes, Luger shoved Sting to the mat. "I couldn't believe Lex's arrogance," Sting told reporters after the match. "The first words out of his mouth were, 'You'll never beat me, not in a million years.' I just said, 'What's your problem? Do something! Come at me!' Well, he did, and the battle was on."

Sting and Luger brawled in a corner of the ring. They tore into each other with fists and kicks. Sting splashed Luger to the mat, but Luger came back and rocked Sting with a clothesline that nearly knocked the wind out of him.

"I've never been so shocked in my life," Sting said later. "I've never had an opponent shake off my splash so easily, but Luger came out and nearly took my head off with that clothesline." Sting was in trouble. Luger whipped him into the ropes and slammed him to the mat. The sound of the impact echoed through the arena. Then Luger signaled to the crowd that he was about to lift Sting into his "human torture rack" backbreaker. Sting got free, picked up Luger, and slammed him backwards onto the mat. With this move, known as a suplex, Sting regained the advantage.

The two combatants traded the advantage several times as the intensity heightened. Sting resorted to illegal tactics, raking his fingers across Luger's eyes. He lifted Luger and dropped him neck-first onto the top rope. Luger was wobbly, but Sting made a mistake when he missed a splash and flew over the top rope. Luger pursued him outside the ring and

Pain is imminent as Sting dives toward a downed opponent.

rammed his head into the metal barrier that separated the fans from the ring. Referee Nick Patrick ordered Luger back into the ring. Luger complied, but Harley Race tried to piledrive Sting onto the arena floor. Sting reversed the attempt and sent Race crashing to the mat. As Luger argued with the referee, Sting climbed to the top rope and leaped off, catching Luger across the chest in a flying body press. Luger was defenseless. Sting covered him for the pin. Patrick made the three-count. Sting had regained the world title.

"I was just so filled with adrenaline and passion," Sting said. "The guy's sour attitude really cheeses me off. I really hope I taught the guy a lesson tonight."

Perhaps he had. A few days later, Luger announced that he was leaving WCW and joining the new World Bodybuilding Federation. Still, there was no shortage of challengers. Sting barely survived a title defense against six-foot, five-inch, 450-pound Big Van Vader, a vicious killer who enjoyed hurting his opponents. In April, Sting came out of his match against Vader with cracked ribs and a bruised spleen. At Beach Blast on June 20, 1992, in Mobile, Alabama, Sting pinned Cactus Jack in a violent falls-count-anywhere match.

But more violence awaited Sting. On July 12, Sting squared off against Vader in the main event of the Great American

Bash in Albany, Georgia. Vader, who was managed by Harley Race, was ruthless in his attacks, but Sting cost himself the match. With Vader slumped against the turnbuckle, Sting attempted to execute his Stinger splash. Vader ducked out of the way, and Sting slammed his forehead on a metal hook connecting the turn-buckle to the ringpost. A bloodied Sting fell to the mat.

Vader nearly pinned him, but Sting escaped. Sting got back to his feet, but blood streamed into his eyes. He couldn't see. He swung wildly at Vader and missed. Vader lifted him high, slammed him to the mat, and scored the pin. For the second time, Sting had lost the WCW world championship. "The myth has been destroyed," Race proclaimed. "Vader is the king of athletes, the king of wrestling."

Vader lost the title to Ron Simmons in August but got it back in December. Sting barely survived a feud with Jake "the Snake" Roberts, who several times unleashed his pet cobra on Sting, then went after Vader. In a match on March 11, 1993, in London, England, Sting beat Vader to win his third WCW world title.

"My ribs still hurt from what he did to me last April and my pride is still hurt from what he did to me last July," Sting said. "I've had some victories over Vader since then, but none mean quite as much as this. Watching him wear that belt was

Sting grimaces in pain while in the throes of a figure-four leglock.

more painful than anything else, and having it back makes the hurt disappear. This victory is for the whole world! Vader's done enough damage."

Vader vowed to regain the title, and was true to his promise. Sting didn't even get back to the United States with the belt. On March 17, at a match in Dublin, Ireland, Vader took advantage of assistance from

Harley Race, who also began attacking Sting, to win the world championship.

"When you wrestle Vader, you're also wrestling Race," Sting said. "That's a pretty difficult combination to beat. I'm just proud that I beat him fair and square."

Sting had the right to be proud of being WCW world champion three times. But his pride would have to last him a while. He wouldn't taste world championship glory again for a long time.

5 Downtime

Just because Sting was no longer WCW world champion didn't mean he was no longer in the headlines. He still wrestled in main events, and he fought numerous matches against Vader. When WCW made its first appearance at Madison Square Garden's Paramount Theater on April 14, 1993, Sting was in the main event, and he beat Vader by disqualification. On May 3, 1993, Sting made news again when he and World Wrestling Federation (WWF) superstar Hulk Hogan wrestled on the

Although Sting was no longer WCW world champion, his inimitable style still managed to attract attention.

same card in Japan, although not against each other. It was the first time Sting and Hogan had ever been on the same card.

Sting got some revenge against Vader when he and Davey Boy Smith teamed to beat Vader and Sid Vicious at Beach Bash on July 18, 1993, in Biloxi, Mississippi. "This was a great match for the Stinger and I," Smith said, "and I think we proved once again that the Masters of the Power Bomb aren't so masterful after all."

At Clash of the Champions XXIV on August 18 in Daytona Beach, Florida, Sting teamed with his former rival, Ric Flair, to beat the Colossal Kongs. Sting also beat Flair by countout in an outstanding match that lasted for forty minutes.

Life was going well for Sting in and out of the ring. In late 1993, Sting signed to appear in several episodes of the television show *Thunder in Paradise*, starring fellow wrestling star Hogan. "You never know, maybe we'll both be up for Emmys if this whole thing works out," Sting said.

Sting didn't win an Emmy (an award for excellence in television), but he did team with Road Warrior Hawk to beat WCW world tag team champions the Nasty Boys. They won by disqualification at Starrcade '93 on December 27, 1993, in Charlotte, North Carolina. Sting also finished second in the voting for Most Popular Wrestler of the Year. The winner was Lex Luger, who had become a fan favorite in the WWF.

Sting renewed his feud with Rick Rude. At SuperBrawl IV on February 20, 1994, in Albany, Georgia, Sting, Brian Pillman, and Dusty Rhodes beat Paul Orndorff, Steve Austin, and Rude in a cage match, which is a match fought entirely within a steel cage. Rude attacked Sting after the match and again days later at a television taping of a WCW card. Rude's manager, Harley Race, was again in the opposite corner when Sting took on Rude at Spring Stampede on April 17 in Rosemont, Illinois, but Race accidentally hit Rude with a chair and Sting scored the pin. On May 22, Sting again met up with Vader in Philadelphia and pinned him in the main event of Slamboree.

There was no doubt that even though Sting wasn't world champion, he was one of the best wrestlers in the world. Each year, *Pro Wrestling Illustrated* compiled its rankings of the top 500 wrestlers in the world. In 1991, Sting finished fifth. In 1992, he was number one. In 1993, he was number five. In 1994, he fell to number eight, but he rose to number three in 1995. Sting was the only wrestler to make the top ten six years in a row.

But Sting didn't have what he wanted: the world title. And it seemed to move farther and farther away. Hulk Hogan's arrival in the federation in 1994 drew attention away from Sting, who had been WCW's top fan favorite. Suddenly, Hogan was hearing all the cheers, which got louder when he beat Flair for the world title in July. Promoters were paying more attention to Hogan than they were to Sting.

At Fall Brawl '94 on September 18 in Roanoke, Virginia, Sting, Vader, and the Guardian Angel met in a three-way match to determine the number-one contender for the world title. While the referee was distracted, Vader power-bombed Sting to win the match. Sting was relegated to grudge matches against Big Bubba Rogers, while Flair, Vader, Brutus Beefcake, and others got the title shots. Sting won his second U.S. title by beating Meng on June 18, 1995, but it was hardly a consolation prize.

Sting plays to the crowd, much to the appreciation of his many fans.

Certainly, there were moments of glory for Sting. The Four Horsemen reunited at Halloween Havoc on October 29, 1995, and double-crossed Sting, but the Stinger sought immediate revenge by forcing Flair to submit to his scorpion death lock. Lex Luger returned to WCW, and Sting teamed with the Total Package (Luger) to beat Harlem Heat (the team of Booker T and

Stevie Ray) for the world tag team title on January 22, 1996, in Las Vegas. They lost the belts to Harlem Heat five months later.

By no means was Sting out of the spotlight. He was definitely still a superstar. But he wanted, more than anything else, to be at the center of the action. He wanted to be the man who carried the flag for WCW. Sting should have been careful about what he wished for. Much to his chagrin, he got it.

Whose Side Are You On?

In 1996, the war between WCW and the WWF, the top two federations in North America, was in full swing. WCW's *Nitro* and the WWF's *Raw* were going head-to-head on cable television every Monday night, and many wrestling fans were more interested in who was winning the competition for television ratings than who was winning in the ring. So, on Memorial Day 1996, when Scott Hall—formerly known as Razor Ramon in the WWF—invaded WCW, many people thought he had arrived to do the WWF's bidding. His plans, it turned out, were far more sinister than that.

Hall promised WCW a big surprise and pledged that other famous wrestlers would soon join him. Sting stood up to him, saying, "This is WCW! You're in the jungle, baby." When Hall flicked his toothpick at Sting, Sting slapped him across the face.

Questions about Hall's friends were answered at the Great American Bash on June 16, 1996, in Baltimore. With Kevin Nash, another former WWF wrestler, Hall confronted WCW senior vice president Eric Bischoff, and demanded a match against the three best wrestlers in WCW. When Bischoff told them they would have to wait to find out the names of their opponents, Hall punched Bischoff in the stomach, and Nash power-bombed him through the stage.

Nash and Hall called themselves the Outsiders—WWF invaders set on taking over WCW. During the next few weeks, they learned that their opponents at Bash at the Beach on July 7, 1996, in Daytona Beach, Florida, would be Sting, Luger, and Randy Savage. Nash and Hall, however, refused to reveal the identity of their third teammate.

As the match started, the Outsiders still didn't have their third teammate. Luger was hurt early in the match, so Savage and Sting battled Hall and Nash two-on-two. As Luger was being carried from the ring on a stretcher, Hulk Hogan walked down the aisle. The television announcers and most fans thought he was there to help Sting and Savage, but instead, he climbed into the ring and started legdropping Savage, who was down on the mat. Then he high-fived Nash and Hall. The crowd was shocked. Fans threw trash and drinks into the ring. As Hogan criticized the fans, Hall and Nash stood by and laughed.

"This is a dark day for wrestling," Sting said. "If you can't trust Hulk, who can you trust?" The next night on *Nitro*, Sting told Hogan: "What happened last night, I am not surprised about coming from the two Outsiders. But, I will say I am very, very surprised at you, Hulk Hogan. I should have known when I looked into your eyes. You know something, I made a mistake. But you made a bigger mistake. Because last night you wiped out and trashed every little kid, every single person that was a part of your life, who patterned their lives after you. You told them to say their prayers and to take their vitamins. You told them to believe in themselves. You know something? It's a good thing you told them to believe in themselves because they sure as heck can't believe in you."

Hall, Nash, and Hogan called themselves the New World Order (NWO) and started recruiting new members. Sting was WCW's flag-bearer in this war. At Hog Wild on August 10, 1996, in Sturgis, North Dakota, Sting and Luger lost to Hall and Nash. The NWO tried to recruit Sting and even hired another wrestler to pose as Sting. But when people started asking him, "Who's side are you on?" the real Sting refused to answer.

Then, on September 9, 1996 on *Nitro*, the impostor Sting attacked Luger. Sting couldn't believe that his friends and the fans really thought he had defected to the NWO and had attacked Luger. He was offended by their lack of trust in him. At Fall Brawl on September 15, 1996, in Winston-Salem, North Carolina, Sting, Flair, Luger, and Arn Anderson battled Nash, Hogan, Hall, and the impostor Sting. Sting turned his back on his teammates and walked away. The next night on *Nitro*, Sting had his back turned from the camera when he said, "I carried the WCW banner. I have given my blood, my sweat, and my tears for WCW. So for all those fans out there, and all those wrestlers, and people that never doubted the Stinger, I'll stand by you if you stand by me. But for all the people, all of the commentators, all of the wrestlers, and all of the best friends who did doubt me, you can stick it. From now on, I consider myself a free agent."

A few weeks later, Sting turned down an offer to join the NWO. Over the following months, he never wrestled, and occasionally he was seen in the upper levels of WCW arenas wearing a black trench coat and carrying a baseball bat. The colorful face paint was gone, replaced by a mask of white paint. Sometimes he confronted the NWO, sometimes he'd drop down from the rafters using a rope and offer to help his friends. One night he handed Luger a baseball bat and left without saying anything. When Rick Steiner accused Sting of being anti-WCW, Sting responded by saying nothing and

When Rick Steiner accused Sting of being anti-WCW, Sting responded by slamming him to the mat.

slamming him to the mat. Nobody knew whose side he was on.

Sting's hair grew longer. His mood got darker. Then, on March 16, 1997, in Charleston, South Carolina, Sting made it clear whose side he wasn't on. The main event of Uncensored '97 was a three-way tag team match involving Team NOW (consisting of Hogan, Hall, Nash, and Randy Savage), Team Piper (Roddy Piper, Jeff Jarrett, Chris Benoit, and Steve McMichael), and Team WCW (the Giant, Lex Luger, and Rick and Scott Steiner). Immediately after the match ended, Sting entered the ring by dropping from the ceiling of the arena on a cable and attacked Hall with a baseball bat. Nash

Rick Steiner and Sting continue their brawl outside of the ring.

was next. Sting whacked him across the knees with the bat. Savage joined the fray, and Sting nailed him across the stomach with the bat.

Sting then turned to Hogan, who was standing at ringside with Dennis Rodman of the National Basketball Association's (NBA) Chicago Bulls. Hogan told Sting to drop the bat before he climbed into the ring. Sting complied. The fans' cheers filled the arena as Sting and Hogan squared off. Sting kicked and punched Hogan, then sent him crashing to the mat. Hogan had to be helped back to the dressing room.

"I can't believe Sting would be stupid enough to attack the NWO," said NWO leader Eric Bischoff. "First he turns his back on the fans and WCW, now he attacks the NWO. I think Sting's spent too much time hanging in the rafters. We offered to take him, but now we'll destroy him."

But was Sting on WCW's side? Not exactly. He resisted efforts to join the ranks of the WCW wrestlers. He refused to wrestle. WCW executive committee chairman J. J. Dillon offered Sting a list of top men to wrestle, but Sting refused the offer. "What do you want?" Dillon asked Sting.

His answer was simple: He wanted Hogan. He wanted to be WCW world champion again. And if he couldn't have Hogan, he didn't want anyone.

7 Unstoppable

Sting's match against Hulk Hogan was scheduled for December 28, 1997, at Starrcade in Washington, D.C. During the weeks leading up to the big event, Hogan did everything in his power to try to psychologically distract Sting. The NWO brutalized a life-sized Sting mannequin. But Sting refused to lose focus.

As he made his way to the ring, Sting stared straight ahead and refused to slap hands with the fans. When he got into the ring, he pointed his baseball bat at Hogan, who tossed his bandanna in Sting's face. Sting slapped him across the face. The bell rang. Hogan unleashed a furious assault of kicks and punches that had observers wondering, "Could Sting come back after fifteen months away from the ring and put up a good fight for the world title?"

Twenty minutes into the match, Bret Hart, who had recently joined WCW, walked to ringside. Hogan continued his assault by kicking Sting in the face. With Sting down on the mat, Hogan connected with a legdrop that shook the ring. He grabbed Sting's tights and covered him for the pin. Referee Nick Patrick made the

Sting gets some hang time as he flies toward the mat during a particularly bruising match.

three-count and called for the bell. But the bell didn't ring. Hart had prevented the timekeeper from ringing the bell.

"I said it would never happen again, and it's not going to happen again," said Hart, who a month earlier had been robbed of the WWF world title. Hart felt Patrick, a former member of the NWO, had made a fast three-count. He bounded into the ring, knocked out Patrick, grabbed Hogan, and ordered him to continue the match. Sting beat on his chest and howled to the crowd.

After Sting scored with a Stinger splash, Buff Bagwell and Scott Norton entered the ring on Hogan's behalf. Sting fought them off, then scored with another splash on Hogan, then clamped on the scorpion death lock. Hogan submitted. Hart called for the bell. Sting was a four-time WCW world champion.

"I won. Everybody knows it," Hogan complained. Two weeks later, on January 8, 1998, WCW executive J. J. Dillon ordered Sting to give up the world title and declared it vacant. A rematch would be held to decide who was champion. "You've got no guts," Sting told Dillon. Then he turned to Hogan. "And you are a dead man," he said.

The rematch was held on February 22, 1998, in San Francisco. This time, Sting pinned Hogan fair and square for his fifth world title.

More controversy resulted when Sting lost the title to Randy Savage on

April 19, 1998, in Denver, Colorado. Referee Charles Robinson was knocked out during the match and couldn't count Sting's pin of Savage. Kevin Nash interfered, slammed Sting, and rolled Savage on top of him for the pin.

Sting finally joined the NWO that spring. Actually, it was the NWO Wolfpac, a group led by Kevin Nash. The NWO had split into the Wolfpac and NWO Hollywood, led by Hulk Hogan. Sting teamed with the Giant to win the WCW world tag team belts from Hall and Nash on May 17, 1998. The Giant, however, joined NWO Hollywood and wanted Sting to join with him. Sting refused, the team broke up, and WCW ordered a singles

Ever the fan favorite,
Sting signs autographs
for two of his many admirers.

match between Sting and the Giant to decide who would own the tag team title. Sting beat the Giant on June 14, 1998, and chose Nash as his partner. They held the belts until July 20, 1998, when they lost to the Giant and Hall.

Sting would complete his remarkable decade by winning two more WCW world titles: from Diamond Dallas Page on April 26, 1999, in Fargo, North Dakota, and from Hogan on September 12, 1999, in Winston-Salem, North Carolina. In 1999, he finished third in the voting for Wrestler of the Year. For a brief time, he was even president of WCW. He won that honor by beating Flair on July 19, in Rockford, Illinois. Shortly afterward, Sting gave up the presidency of WCW. He feuded with Bret Hart, Lex Luger, and Vampiro, a former ally. And in early 2000, he appeared to have won the world title from Jeff Jarrett, only to have an official rule that Jarrett's belt wasn't on the line.

The Stinger's career nearly came to a tragic conclusion at the Great American Bash on June 11, 2000, in Baltimore. Sting and Vampiro were battling on top of the Jumbotron screen during a "human torch" match when Sting was set on fire. In a panic, Sting fell off the Jumbotron and through the stage below. He suffered serious burns, but he returned to the ring a month later wearing a ski mask and goggles.

With his dynamic personality and ever-changing personas, Sting has evolved into the quintessential wrestling champ.

Countless times before, Sting had proven to the world that he couldn't be stopped and that if he ever decided to stop wrestling, he would do so on his terms. He is truly one of the top superstars in wrestling history: a colorful, exciting, and talented individual who's the center of attention wherever he goes. The greatness of the Stinger can never be denied.

Glossary

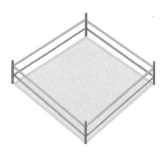

backbreaker   Offensive maneuver in which the attacker lifts his opponent and drops him back-first across his knee.

clique   Small, exclusive group of people; for example, in pro wrestling, the New World Order and the Four Horsemen.

clothesline   Offensive maneuver in which the attacker sticks out his arm and jams it against his opponent's neck.

disqualification   Ruling by the referee in which a wrestler automatically loses a match for violating a rule.

draw   In wrestling, a match in which neither wrestler wins; a tie.

feud   Series of matches between two wrestlers or two tag teams. Many times one wrestler will bad-mouth the other wrestler or will sneak attack the wrestler.

figure-four leglock   Submission move in which the attacker wraps his leg around and inside his opponent's legs and applies pressure on the thighs and lower back.

flying body press Move in which a wrestler leaps off the ropes and catches an opponent across the chest with his own chest.

main event Featured match at a wrestling show, usually the last match of the night.

pin When either both shoulders or both shoulder blades are held in contact with the mat for three continuous seconds. Also called a pinfall. A pin ends a match.

power-bomb Move in which a wrestler lifts an opponent upside down and drives the opponent's shoulders into the mat.

promoter Person or people responsible for financing and organizing a wrestling show or event.

submission hold Move that makes an opponent give up without being pinned.

tag team match Match involving two teams of two or more wrestlers. Only one wrestler from each team is allowed in the ring at a time.

turnbuckle The padded area where the ropes meet in all four corners of a wrestling ring.

For More Information

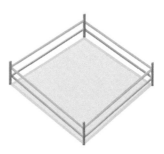

Magazines

Pro Wrestling Illustrated, The Wrestler, Inside Wrestling, Wrestle America, and *Wrestling Superstars*
London Publishing Co.
7002 West Butler Pike
Ambler, PA 19002

WCW Magazine
P.O. Box 420235
Palm Coast, FL 32142-0235

WOW Magazine
McMillen Communications
P.O. Box 500
Missouri City, TX 77459-9904
e-mail: woworder@mcmillencomm.com
Web site: http://www.wowmagazine.com

Web Sites

Powerslam's Sting Site
http://www.geocities.com/jfjwrestling/
   sting

Professional Wrestling Online Museum
http://www.wrestlingmuseum.com

Pro Wrestling Torch Newsletter
http://www.pwtorch.com

World Championship Wrestling
http://www.wcw.com

World Wrestling Federation
http://www.wwf.com

For Further Reading

Albano, Lou, Bert Randolph Sugar, and
    Michael Benson. *The Complete
    Idiot's Guide to Pro Wrestling*.
    2nd ed. New York: Alpha Books, 2000.

Archer, Jeff. *Theater in a Squared
    Circle*. New York: White-Boucke
    Publishing, 1998.

Cohen, Dan. *Wrestling Renegades:
    An In-Depth Look at Today's*

Superstars of Pro Wrestling. New York: Archway, 1999.

Conner, Floyd. *Wrestling's Most Wanted: The Top 10 Book of Pro Wrestling's Outrageous Performers, Punishing Piledrivers, and Other Oddities.* Washington, D.C.: Brassey's Inc., 2001.

Hofstede, David. *Slammin': Wrestling's Greatest Heroes and Villains.* New York: ECW Press, 1999.

Mazer, Sharon. *Professional Wrestling: Sport and Spectacle.* Jackson, MS: University Press of Mississippi, 1998.

Myers, Robert. *The Professional Wrestling Trivia Book.* Boston, MA: Branden Books, 1999.

Works Cited

Apter, Bill. "Superstar Summit: Sting and Hogan Said It, *PWI* Reveals It!" *Pro Wrestling Illustrated*, September 1993, pp. 43–45.

Rosenbaum, David. "Outlook for Sting: Bright and Sunny. Forecast for Lex Luger: Reign Ending!" *Pro Wrestling Illustrated,* April 1992, pp. 35–37.

Smith, Bob. "Sting Wins the NWA World Title!" *Pro Wrestling Illustrated*, November 1990, pp. 86–93.

"Sting Prognosis: Out Until August."
Pro Wrestling Illustrated Weekly,
March 5, 1990, p. 1.

"Sting Vs. Hogan: The Match of the
Century." *Pro Wrestling Illustrated*,
February 1998, pp. 25–27.

"The State of Sting." *The Wrestler
Presents Greats of the Game*,
April 2001, pp. 62–93.

Index

Photo Credits

All photos © Colin Bowman.

Series Design and Layout

Geri Giordano